The big 5
and other wild animals

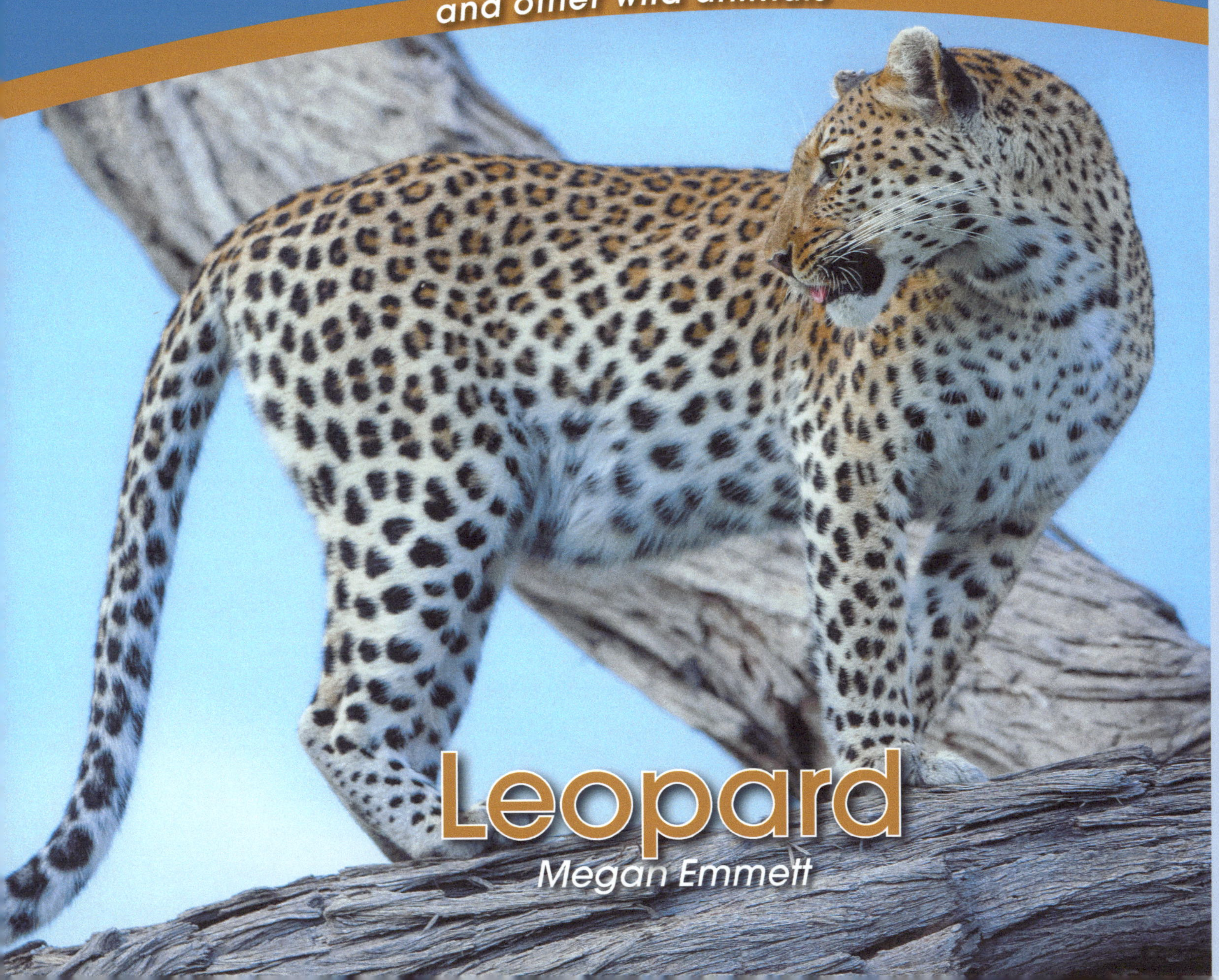

Leopard
Megan Emmett

The big 5 and other wild animals series is published by
Awareness Publishing Group (Pty) Ltd.
Copyright © 2019

Awareness Publishing (SA) (Pty) Ltd
www.awareness.co.za
info@awareness.co.za
+27 (0)86 110 1491
www.facebook.com/AwarenessPublishing

All rights reserved. No part of this publication may be reproduced in any form without written permission from the publisher, except by a reviewer.

First edition, 2019

Leopard by Megan Emmett
ISBN 978-0-6393-0004-7

Summary: An introduction to the leopard, one of the Big Five wild animals. This book looks at the leopard's physical characteristics, its territory, and its hunting and eating habits. The book also talks about the conservation of leopards.

Book design: Dana Espag and Bianca Keenan-Smith.

Editorial credits: Educational consultant: Gillian Mervis. Copy editor: Danya Ristić. Proofreader: Lynda Gilfillan. Picture editor: Anne Laing. Indexer: Lois C Henderson.

Illustrations: Cartoons: Gerhard Cruywagen of Greenhouse Cartoons, and Dana Espag.

Photo credits: Cover and pp.3 (top and middle), 8, 12, 13, 15, 22, 26, 28, 32, 35 (bottom), 37, 44, and 48 © Shem Compion; p.3 (bottom) © funkyjunky / iStockphoto; p.4 © AfriPics; p.6 © Wolfgang_Steiner; p.7 © Moodboard_Images / iStockphoto; p.8 (inset) © BjornRasmussen / iStockphoto; p.9 (left) © South African Tourism; (right) © Anne Laing; p.10 © John Conrad / Great Stock / Corbis; p.14 © Heinrich van den Berg / Gallo Images; p.16 © lienkie / iStockphoto; pp.17 and 23 (top and bottom) © Megan Emmett; p.18 (left) © Terraxplorer / iStockphoto; (right) © GJohnson2 / iStockphoto; p.20 (inset) © Andrew Chislett; © Barbra Leigh / Great Stock / Corbis; p.24 © tammielsmith / iStockphoto; p.25 (top and bottom) © RollingEarth / iStockphoto; p.27 © Nigel Dennis / Gallo Images; p.30 © Daleen Loest / Shutterstock; p.31 (top) © Lynn Newby-Fraser; (bottom left) © pjmalsbury / iStockphoto; (middle) © Raphael Melnick / Wikipedia; (right) © javarman3 / iStockphoto; p.33 © Freder / iStockphoto; p.34 © GP232 / iStockphoto; p.35 (top) © davidwarshaw / iStockphoto; (middle) © VilliersSteyn / iStockphoto; p.36 © Prof Lee Berger; p.38 (top) © amuren / iStockphoto; (bottom) © Megan Emmett / Aquavision; p.40 (top) © imagewerks / iStockphoto; (bottom) © pjmalsbury / iStockphoto; p.41 © pjmalsbury / iStockphoto; p.42 © Rajesh Jantilal / Gallo Images; p.45 © David Goldblatt / Africa Media Online; p.46 © Alamy Images / AfriPics; p.50 © davidwarshaw / iStockphoto.

You can read more by Megan Emmett about animals in the book *Game Ranger in Your Backpack – All-in-one Interpretative Guide to the Lowveld*, published by Briza Publications (2010, Pretoria). ISBN 978-1-920217-06-8.

1 3 5 7 9 0 8 6 4 2

Contents

Quick facts 5
What is a leopard? 7
Lots of spots 9
Leopards with no spots 11
Where does a leopard live? 13
Why leopards have territories 15
Marking a territory 17
Tough bodies 19
Sharp claws 21
Paws 23
Sharp sight 25
What leopards hunt 27
What leopards eat 29
Food in trees 31
Cubs 33
Growing up 35
"Follow me" signs 37
Mating and pregnancy 39
Habits 41
Cultural uses 43
People and leopards 45
Conservation 47
Glossary 49

Leopards often climb trees.

Quick facts

Height (at the shoulder)	Male: 70–80 centimetres Female: 60–70 centimetres
Weight	Male: 60–90 kilograms Female: 30–60 kilograms
Lifespan	11–15 years (20 at the most)
Gestation (pregnancy)	About 100 days (just over three months)
Number of young	Two or three
Habitat	Many areas, as long as they have good hiding places
Food	Mainly antelope such as impala, but also other creatures such as mice, lizards, snakes and fish, as well as small carnivores, or meat-eaters
Predators	Cubs are killed by lions and spotted hyena
Interesting fact	Male leopards are also known as *toms*
Is it one of the Big Five?	Yes!

Words that appear in the text in bold, **like this**, are explained in the Glossary at the end of this book. Some key words are in colour.

A leopard feeding on prey that it has carried up a tree.

What is a leopard?

Leopards are big cats, and are part of the same family as a house cat. In the African wild, there are three kinds of big cats: lions, leopards and cheetahs. Leopards are smaller than lions, but bigger than cheetahs. All three kinds of cats are powerful animals. Leopards have especially large muscles in their shoulders, to help them climb trees and jump onto their **prey**, which are the animals that they eat.

Two leopards in a tree, carefully watching people who are watching them.

Leopards are **predators** – they hunt and kill other animals. They usually eat antelope and warthogs, but also monkeys, baboons, birds and other small animals. They even eat fish.

Leopards are part of a group of animals that we call the Big Five. These are the biggest and most dangerous animals in the wild. The other animals that make up the Big Five are lion, rhino, elephant and buffalo. Long ago, people from Europe used to come to Africa to hunt the Big Five because they wanted to prove and show how brave they were. Nowadays, many people go on holiday to a game reserve to see the Big Five, and leopard is one of the animals they want to see the most.

Leopards are shy, they do not like being with other animals or people, so it is often difficult to see them.

A leopard's spots help it to hide in grass and bush.

Rosettes on a leopard's coat.

Lots of spots

We call the fur of an animal its fur coat, or just its coat. The leopard has a shiny, gold-coloured coat that is covered with black spots. Each large spot on a leopard is made up of a circle of smaller spots, called a rosette. Leopards' spots are different from cheetahs' spots, which are solid and round.

The rosettes are part of the leopard's camouflage – they help the leopard to hide. Because of the camouflage, the leopard's coat blends in with the leaves of a tree where it hides. So other animals and people cannot see it.

These rosettes also help the leopard when it is catching prey. Leopards hunt animals such as antelope, warthogs and small carnivores, or meat-eaters. These animals run away quickly if they see a leopard coming. The leopard's spots help it to blend in with the grass so that its prey will not see it hiding there. The leopard can then creep up close to the prey and **pounce** on it more easily.

A leopard.

A cheetah.

A black panther.

Leopards with no spots

The spots on a leopard are black because of the **melanin** pigment, or colouring matter, that the animal has in its fur. If a leopard has a lot of melanin in its fur, the whole leopard is black. We call a completely black leopard a black panther. It is still a kind of leopard, just with a different-coloured coat. If you look closely at a panther's black coat, you can see the leopard spots shining through. Panthers are rare animals, and people do not often see them in game reserves.

A leopard stands on a fallen tree, guarding its territory and looking out for prey.

Where does a leopard live?

A **habitat** is the place where an animal lives. Leopards live in many habitats. They may live in forests where there are lots of trees, or they may live in the desert where there are no trees. They may also live in the bushveld, or in swamps, which get a lot of rain.

Leopards live in any place where there is enough food for them to eat. When a leopard finds a place that has plenty of food, it will make that place its **territory**. It will chase away any other leopards that try to come into its territory.

A female leopard stays with her cub until it is fully grown.

Both male and female leopards have their own territories. A male's territory is much bigger than that of a female. Leopards mostly live by themselves, but when it is time to mate, a male leopard will come into the female's territory.

The only time when there is more than one leopard living in a territory is when a female leopard has cubs.

A male leopard stops to watch and listen to something while walking through his territory.

Why leopards have territories

Leopards make sure that other leopards know where their territory is. They do this mainly to avoid fights.

Leopards live on their own, and have to hunt on their own to feed themselves. So a leopard cannot risk getting injured in an unnecessary fight with another leopard. An injured leopard would not be able to hunt properly, and this could mean going hungry or even starving to death.

So leopards make sure to patrol their territory, walking all over it and clearly marking it.

A leopard patrolling its territory.

A leopard rubbing its head against a tree branch.

Marking a territory

Animals have various ways of communicating with other animals. When a leopard makes a territory for itself, it makes certain signs to tell other leopards to keep out. We call this marking territory.

A leopard has several ways of marking its territory. One way is to make a noise. The leopard makes a loud noise that sounds like someone sawing or cutting through a thick piece of wood. It is a deep sound that other leopards can hear even if they are far away.

A leopard spraying urine onto a tree to mark its territory.

Another way a leopard marks its territory is with different smells. Their **dung**, or waste matter, has a strong smell. A leopard leaves its dung in piles where other leopards will see it and smell it. Their urine also has a strong smell. Leopards spray their urine backwards onto bushes and trees, and then they rub their paws in it. As they walk, the smell from their paws stays on the ground and in this way they mark their territory.

Leopards also give off a smell from their cheeks. They leave this smell behind by rubbing their faces on bushes as they walk through their territories.

To carry its prey up into a tree, a leopard holds the prey in its powerful jaws.

Leopards can easily climb up and down trees because their bodies are so strong.

Tough bodies

Each animal's body has special features, called **adaptations**, that help the animal to live easily and comfortably in its habitat. Leopards spend a lot of time sleeping in trees or hiding their prey in trees. Because of this, their bodies are adapted to climbing up and down trees easily. A leopard's adaptations are so good that it can carry prey that is as heavy as its own body.

When a leopard climbs up a tree, it holds its prey in its mouth. This is why leopards have thick, strong necks and big heads with strong jaws. The prey is often large and heavy. It hangs down between the leopard's front legs while the leopard climbs. Another adaptation is that the leopard's chest curves inwards, so the prey that it is carrying does not get in the way.

Because a leopard pulls itself up with its front legs, it has strong shoulders. Leopards also have sharp claws, which help them to climb trees. The dewclaws are special claws that are higher up on the back of the leopards' front paws (see the photograph on page 20). These claws help with climbing because the leopard uses them to hold on to trees.

A leopard's paw, with its sharp claws that it uses to climb trees and catch prey.

A leopard scratches its claws on a tree trunk.

Sharp claws

All cats scratch their claws against solid objects. House cats often scratch a chair in the sitting room. In the wild, leopards scratch their claws against tree trunks. To do this, they stretch their front legs high up on the tree trunk and then drag their claws downwards over the rough bark.

A leopard claws trees for three reasons. First, to leave its claw marks on the tree. This is a way of marking territory. If another leopard comes along and sees the claw marks, it will know that the territory belongs to some other leopard.

Second, clawing trees helps to keep the leopard's claws healthy. The rough bark breaks off any old pieces of claw. It also sharpens the leopard's claws.

Third, leopards need to stretch their bodies. They do this by putting their front paws high up on a tree trunk and then dragging their claws downwards. Stretching is a kind of exercise – it helps to keep leopards fit and healthy so that they can catch their prey.

The soft pads on a leopard's paws help it to walk quietly.

Paws

Predators have special feet that help them to walk quietly, or even silently, when they sneak up on prey. Leopards walk on the tips of their toes, and the back or heel of the paw never touches the ground.

Little cushions or pads on the leopard's paws help it to walk quietly. Leopards can feel the ground under their paws with these pads. They carefully put their paws between twigs, dry branches and clumps of grass so that they do not make a noise and so that their prey does not hear them as they come closer.

The pads leave a print or mark on the ground, showing where the leopard walked. We call this a **track**. Lions are the biggest cats and their tracks are the largest of all the cats. The leopard's track looks much like a lion's track, but it is smaller and rounder. Each leopard track is nine to ten centimetres long.

A leopard's track.

A lion's track.

A leopard's excellent eyesight helps it to hunt.

Sharp sight

Like people, animals have five senses: seeing, smelling, touching, hearing and tasting. A leopard's hearing and sense of smell are important, but it uses its sight the most. Leopards use their excellent eyesight to catch prey during the day and also at night.

At the back of humans' and animals' eyes is something called the retina. Inside the retina there are two kinds of cells, called cones and rods, that react to light. The cones see colour and work best when there is lots of light. The rods see black and white and work best when there is not much light. Leopards have many more rods than cones in their retinas. This means that leopards see well in the dark.

Some animals, such as antelope, have eyes on the sides of their heads. These animals can watch all around for danger. Other animals, such as leopards, have eyes that face or look forwards. These animals cannot see all around. To look around, they must turn their heads. But having eyes that face forwards allows the animal to see how far away things are, and this is good for hunting.

Leopards have forward-facing eyes.

Antelope have eyes on the sides of their heads.

A leopard stalks a herd of impala.

What leopards hunt

When a predator sneaks or creeps up on its prey, we say that it is **stalking**. The predator moves slowly and carefully so that it gets close to its prey without the prey seeing it. It can then attack the prey.

Leopards are the best stalkers of all the cats. Before they pounce on their prey, they often get as close as five metres to the animal. They have to be very patient and move slowly, little by little, towards the prey. If the prey looks up, the leopard freezes, standing completely still.

If the prey sees the predator, it runs away as fast as it can. Often, the predator cannot catch the prey because the prey runs away too quickly. But sometimes the predator gets close enough to the prey before the prey sees it. And then the prey is surprised and it cannot get away in time.

Leopards use their powerful bodies to catch and capture their prey. They grab it with their front claws and pull it to the ground. By biting the animal on the back of the head or around the throat, they are able to kill it.

Whiskers

The long white hairs on the sides of a leopard's nose are its whiskers. These hairs help the leopard when it stalks its prey. The whiskers tell the leopard if a space in the grass or bushes, for example, is big enough for it to fit through. Whiskers also help the leopard to feel around in the dark without bumping into things.

A leopard trying to catch a porcupine.

What leopards eat

Some animals are **opportunists**. They use every chance or opportunity that they get to find food. They usually hunt at night, but when they can, they also catch food during the day. Being opportunists also means that these animals eat whatever kinds of food they find.

Leopards are opportunists. They usually eat antelope such as impala and duiker. But they also eat many other kinds of food, for example termites, fish that are stuck in mud, birds, mice, snakes, porcupines and even baby buffalo.

Leopards are also **scavengers**, because they sometimes steal food from other animals. Unlike lions and hyenas, leopards usually hunt instead of stealing animals that other predators have killed. But leopards do steal fresh **kills** from cheetahs.

Leopards are fussy about what they eat. They pull out the hair or feathers from the animal before eating it. They do not eat the intestines of their prey. They pull the intestines out and cover them with sand or plants, to hide the smell. If scavengers such as lion or hyena smell the kill, they will try to steal it from the leopard.

If a leopard needs to go away from its kill and then come back, it covers the remains, or what is left of the kill, with plants or soil to keep it safe.

A leopard with a piece of prey that it has hoisted up a tree, so that hyenas and lions cannot steal it.

Food in trees

Lion and hyena steal and scavenge food from leopards. To get away from these scavengers, leopards hoist and lift their food into a tree. Hyenas cannot climb trees, and lions are not good climbers, so the leopard and its food are safer up in the tree.

Hyena often wait below the tree, hoping to pick up any scraps or pieces of the leopard's prey. Sometimes, large parts of the kill fall out of the tree. The hyenas eat these quickly and greedily.

In areas where there are few scavengers, leopards feed on the ground, and do not bother to hoist their prey up a tree.

This leopard has hoisted its kill up a tree to get away from the hyena on the ground below.

A cub explores the area around it while it waits for its mother to return from hunting.

Cubs

A leopard's baby is called a **cub**. When cubs are born, they are small and helpless. They cannot open their eyes for about six weeks, so they are blind during this time. To keep them safe until they are a little bigger, the cubs' mother finds hiding places for them. She hides them in thick bushes, in holes between rocks, or in caves. The cubs drink milk, or **suckle**, from her teats. The male leopard does not help to raise the cubs.

Even when the cubs are older, the mother leaves them in hiding places when she goes hunting for food. Once she has caught and killed her prey, she fetches her cubs and takes them to eat from the kill.

A female leopard carries her young cub, gripping it in her mouth. Mothers usually hide their cubs while they go out to hunt.

A mother leopard gives birth to between one and three cubs at a time. We call this a **litter**. When the cubs are on their own, waiting for their mother to return, they spend time playing and exploring, finding out about the area around them.

Playing is not only for fun. It also helps the cubs to exercise their small bodies. They learn how to pounce by jumping on insects or lizards. It is important for them to learn this **skill** so that they can hunt for themselves when they are older.

A female leopard holds her cub back with her paw, so that it does not go too far into the water.

Growing up

All animals are born with **instincts**. This means that they are born knowing how to do certain things without having to learn to do them, and they do these things without thinking. An example of an instinct is that newborn babies immediately know how to suck milk from their mother. Predators kill each other's cubs by instinct. In this way, they make sure that they have fewer enemies and more food to eat. Even though a leopard mother hides her cubs, other predators still find them and kill them. About half of all leopard cubs are killed or die from other causes when they are still young.

Leopard mothers suckle their cubs for the first three months, and then they hunt food for their cubs. When the cubs are just over nine months old, they start going with their mother to learn how to hunt. They make their first kill at around 11 months old.

During the first year, the cubs learn to hunt, but they cannot look after themselves yet. They stay with their mother in her territory. When they are about a year and a half old, they have learnt enough about hunting to leave and find their own territory.

Young adult leopards do not always find a territory of their own straight away. Until they do, their mother allows them to hunt in her territory.

Leopards have white tail-tips, and black fur on the backs of their ears. Cubs look out for their mother's white and black markings while they are following her.

"Follow me" signs

Leopards have long tails with a white tip at the end. The white tip of a mother's tail is a "follow me" sign. When cubs walk with their mother in long grass, the white tip of her tail is easy to follow because it is at a height where they can see it. Another "follow me" sign is the back of the mother's ears, which are black. As the cubs walk behind her, they follow the black fur behind her ears.

Young leopards play together by using the tip of their mother's tail as a target. They pounce on it while they follow her in the long grass. Leopards have long tails because it helps them to balance when they are climbing trees.

The black behind a mother leopard's ears helps her cubs to follow her.

Two leopards mating – the male is on top.

After mating, the male, on the left, is still on top. The female has just tried to swat him, and he raises his paw to protect himself.

Mating and pregnancy

When a female leopard wants to mate, she has different ways of telling the male. She calls him by making lots of sawing sounds. She also leaves her smell, by urinating and dropping dung, wherever she thinks a male will pick up the smell. Sometimes, she even leaves her territory to look for a male.

When she finds a male, they mate every ten minutes for two to five days. When the male withdraws his penis at the end of each mating, this is painful for the female, and she then swats or smacks the male across his face or neck.

The length of time that a female is pregnant is called the **gestation** period. A female leopard is pregnant for three months. The leopard's gestation period is short as compared to some other animals of the same size because it is difficult for the female to move around, and hunt, with a big belly. If her gestation was longer, she could not hunt, and she would starve.

Because female leopards have a short gestation, the cubs are not well developed when they are born. The cubs' eyes are closed and they are helpless. They need to be kept completely safe for the first six weeks, and for several months after that their mother still has to hide them in different places when she goes out to hunt.

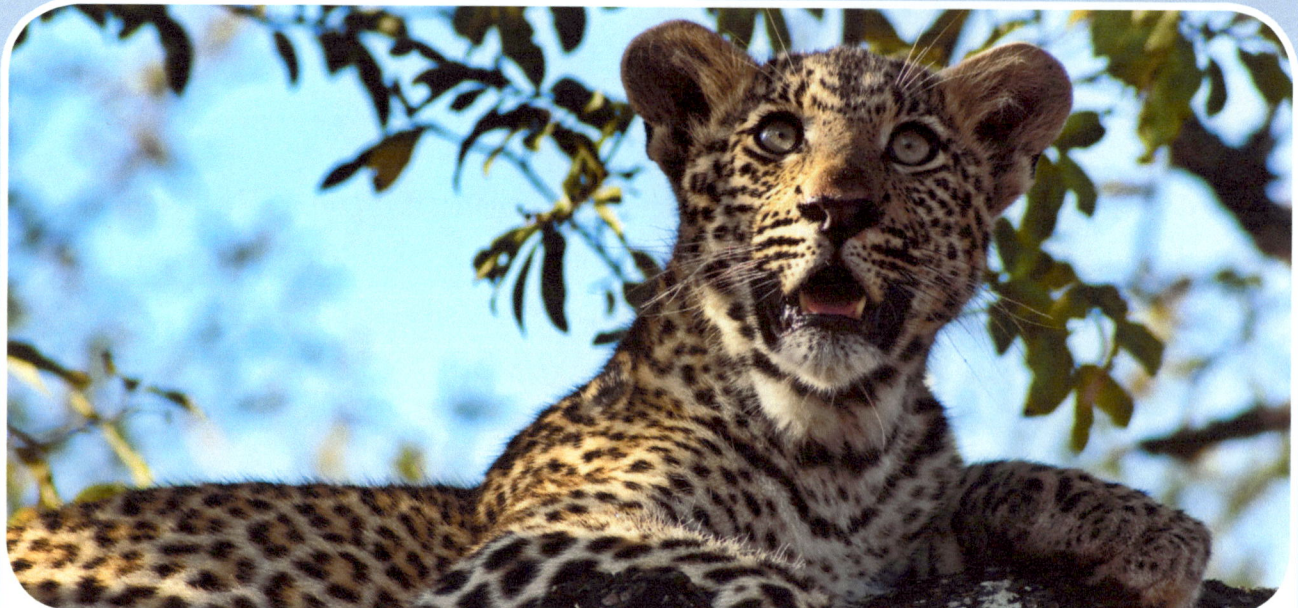
Leopards usually rest at midday. On hot days they lie in shady places, such as in trees.

On cold days, leopards warm up by lying on stones and rocks in the sun.

Habits

A **habit** is something that we do over and over again. Animals have many habits. They almost always act in the same way and do the same things every day.

One habit that leopards have is sleeping in the shade during the middle of the day. Because hunting makes them tired, they save their energy by resting when it is hot. Resting gives them strength to hunt later. They tend to hunt at night, when it is cooler. During the day, they usually rest in the bushes along a river, or in a leafy tree. They may also go into a cave to rest.

Another habit that leopards have is lying on rocks in the sun when the weather is cold. This helps them to warm their bodies.

Leopards have a habit of rolling in the dung of other animals. Nobody knows exactly why they do this. The smell of the dung may help to hide the leopard's own smell when it is hunting. Or it could be a way of marking territory. The leopard's own smell would go onto the dung and then other leopards would know that this territory belongs to another leopard.

Grooming

Leopards lick their paws and other parts of their bodies that they can reach. They do this to get rid of dirt and dried blood after feeding. Leopards spend a lot of time grooming themselves because they like to be clean. A mother and her cubs groom one another in the places that are hard to reach.

President Jacob Zuma and his wife, Thobeka, wore leopard skins at their wedding in 2010.

Cultural uses

Many people hunt leopards for these animals' skins. In some cultures in Africa, people sew clothes, called capes, from leopard skin. The king and other important people then wear the capes around their shoulders. Sometimes, people make costumes from leopard skins for religious **ceremonies**, or special events.

In Central and West Africa, people sell leopard skins and teeth at markets. The skins and teeth are used for traditional **rituals** and religious ceremonies. In China, leopard bones are used in traditional healing.

In some cultures young men are supposed to kill a leopard to show that they have grown up and are now adults. People also use leopards' whiskers to make medicines.

Leopards have to watch out for danger at all times, such as when they drink water.

People and leopards

Sometimes people kill leopards, for various reasons.

One reason is the competition between leopards and humans living in the same area. When people cut down bush or forests to make way for new towns or to use the wood, the places that are left for leopards to live and hunt in become smaller. In this way, people change the leopards' habitat. There is less space for leopards to live in, so there is less food for them to eat. The leopards then come looking for food around people's homes, and steal their sheep or goats, so the people kill the leopards. Sometimes farmers set leopard-killing traps so that the leopards can no longer hunt their animals.

A stuffed leopard. This leopard is no longer alive, it has been killed and stuffed. Some people kill leopards to show off the stuffed animal in their home.

Some people are afraid of leopards, and so they kill them. Other people hunt leopards for their skins or because they want to show off the stuffed animal in their home. To do this, a hunter must first get a permit. Hunting leopards without a permit is not allowed, and is illegal.

At times, farmers may also kill leopards by mistake, by poisoning them. Jackals hunt sheep from farms. A farmer may try to kill a jackal by putting poison into some meat and leaving the meat lying around the farm for the jackal to eat. A leopard may find and eat the meat before the jackal does, and may die instead of the jackal.

A leopard in a game reserve, where people can see it without harming it.

Conservation

When we conserve wildlife, we protect wild animals and the places where these animals live.

Leopards can survive well in the wild, so we say that they are a successful **species**. They live in the wild and also in game reserves. But there are not as many leopards as there once were, because people are hunting and killing them.

Leopards manage to stay alive because of certain things that they do: they hide from humans. They eat whatever they can find. They run fast and stalk their prey quietly. They climb high up into trees. They live in many different places – from deserts to forests.

It is difficult to count how many leopards are left in Africa. Some people think there are about 700 000, while other people say that there are only 10 000. Whatever the number is, there are fewer leopards nowadays than there used to be, and the number gets smaller every year. The number of places where leopards can live also gets smaller every year. Because of this, we say that leopards are near threatened. They may become endangered if their number keeps getting smaller. If an animal is endangered, it may die off and become extinct. Then there would be no leopards left in the world at all.

Many people are studying leopards to try to learn more about them, so that we can look after them and conserve them.

Leopards keep safe by climbing high up in trees.

Glossary

adaptations – special features in an animal's body that make it easier for the animal to live in its habitat

camouflage – the colours or patterns on an animal's coat that help the animal to blend in with plants and other things around it, so that it cannot be seen

ceremonies – religious events that celebrate a particular happening or something special that someone has done

dung – an animal's solid waste matter

gestation – the length of time that a female is pregnant

habit – something that people and animals repeat or do over and over again

habitat – the larger area where an animal lives

instincts – things that animals know how to do without needing to learn them or think about doing them

kills – animals that a predator has killed for food

litter – a group of baby animals that are born at one time to one mother

melanin – the pigment, or colouring matter, that makes an animal's fur a certain colour, either just in places or all over

opportunists – animals that take every opportunity or chance to hunt for food, and that eat whatever food they find

Leopard cubs climb trees as soon as they are able to do so.

Glossary continued

pounce – to jump quickly on something to catch it

predators – animals that hunt and kill other animals for food

prey – animals that are hunted and killed by other animals for food

rituals – ceremonies or religious events at which things must be done in a certain way; these things are always repeated in the same order

scavengers – animals that steal food from other animals, or eat pieces of a kill that the killer has not eaten

skill – something that people and animals learn to do by practising doing it

species – animals of the same type, which can breed with each other

stalking – creeping or sneaking up slowly

suckle – to feed by drinking milk from the mother's teats

territory – the specific area where only one animal, or group of animals, lives

track – the marks or prints of an animal's feet showing where the animal walked

www.ingramcontent.com/pod-product-compliance
Lightning Source LLC
Chambersburg PA
CBHW041322290426

44108CB00004B/107